EASY GUITAR
WITH NOTES & TAB

once

## contents

ISBN 978-1-4768-7132-5

HAL•LEONARD®
CORPORATION
7777 W. BLUEMOUND RD. P.O. BOX 13819 MILWAUKEE, WI 53213

In Australia Contact:
Hal Leonard Australia Pty. Ltd.
4 Lentara Court
Cheltenham, Victoria, 3192 Australia
Email: ausadmin@halleonard.com.au

Visit Hal Leonard Online at
www.halleonard.com

# STRUM AND PICK PATTERNS

This chart contains the suggested strum and pick patterns that are referred to by number at the beginning of each song in this book. The symbols ⊓ and ∨ in the strum patterns refer to down and up strokes, respectively. The letters in the pick patterns indicate which right-hand fingers play which strings.

**p = thumb**
**i = index finger**
**m = middle finger**
**a = ring finger**

For example; Pick Pattern 2
is played: thumb - index - middle - ring

## Strum Patterns          ## Pick Patterns

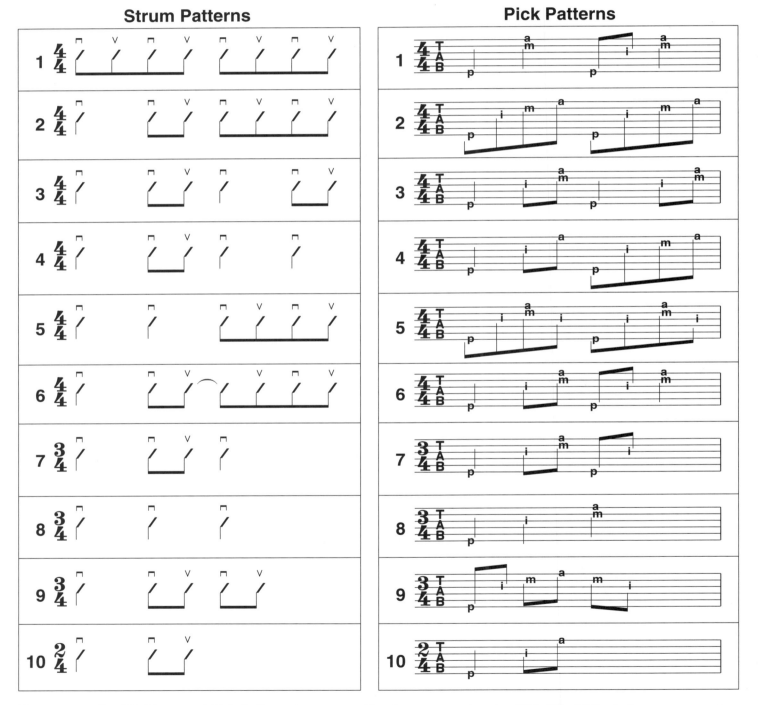

You can use the 3/4 Strum and Pick Patterns in songs written in compound meter (6/8, 9/8, 12/8, etc.).
For example, you can accompany a song in 6/8 by playing the 3/4 pattern twice in each measure.
The 4/4 Strum and Pick Patterns can be used for songs written in cut time (¢) by doubling the note
time values in the patterns. Each pattern would therefore last two measures in cut time.

# Falling Slowly

**Words and Music by Glen Hansard and Marketa Irglova**

*Hereafter referred to as Both.*

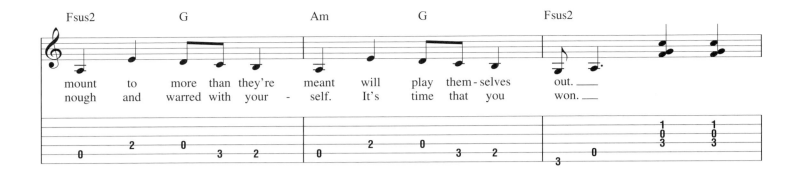

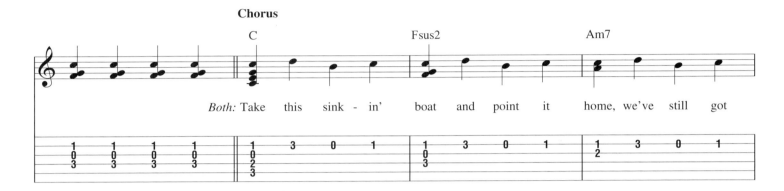

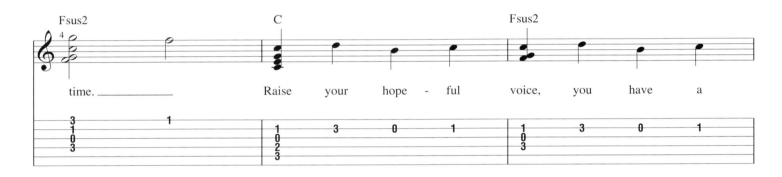

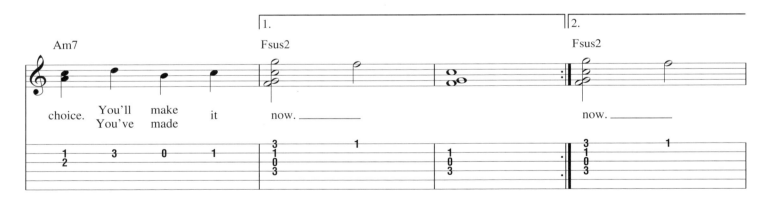

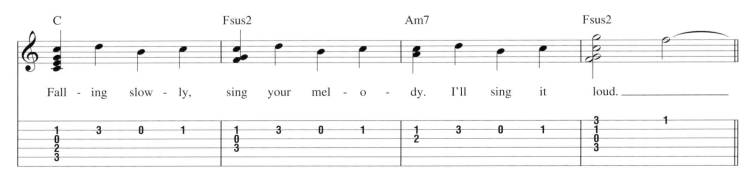

# If You Want Me

### Words and Music by Marketa Irglova

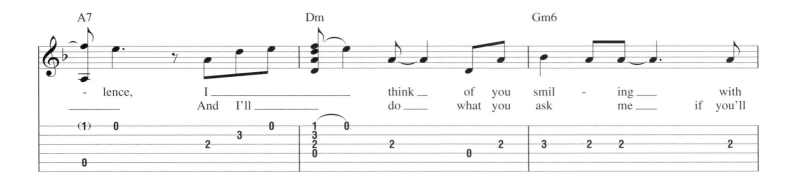

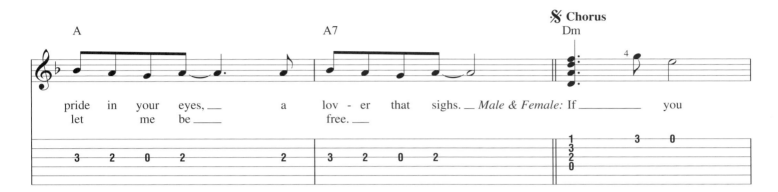

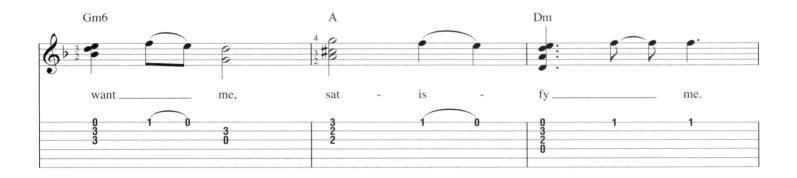

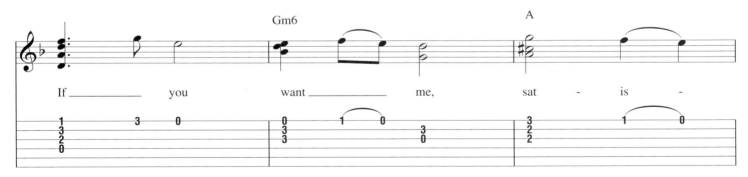

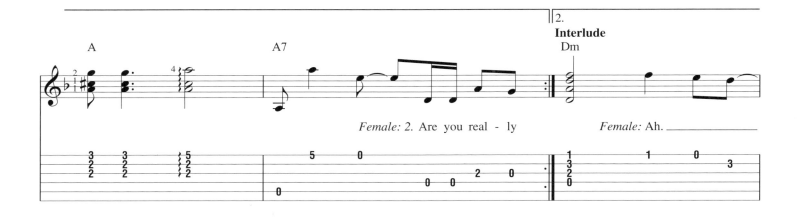

*D.S. al Coda*

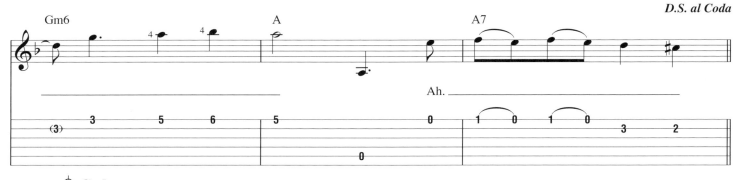

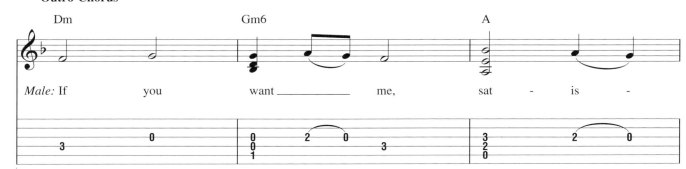

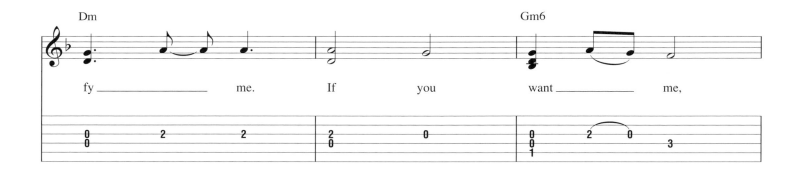

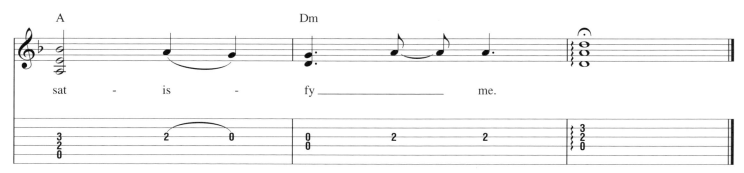

# Lies

**Words and Music by Glen Hansard and Marketa Irglova**

**Strum Pattern: 3**
**Pick Pattern: 5**

tak - in' _____ time _____ to save him - self. The

**Pre-Chorus**

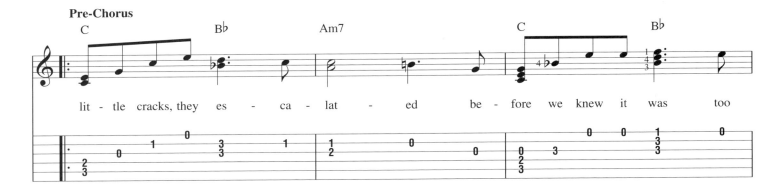

lit - tle cracks, they es - ca - lat - ed be - fore we knew it was too

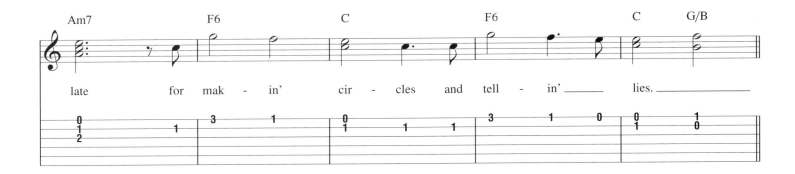

late for mak - in' cir - cles and tell - in' _____ lies. _____

**Chorus**

You're mov - in' too _____ fast for me and I can't keep up _____

_____ with ___ you. May - be if ___ you slowed ___ down for me,

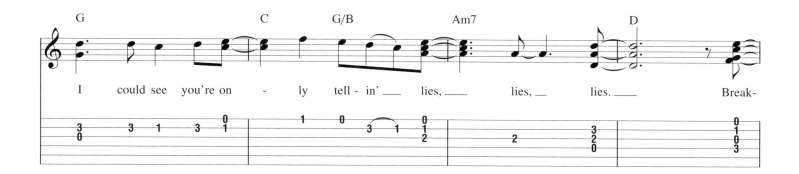

I could see you're on - ly tell - in' ___ lies, ___ lies, ___ lies. ___ Break-

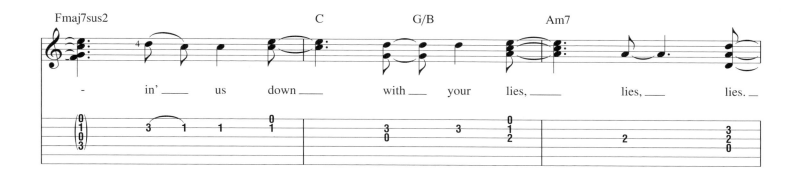

- in' ___ us down ___ with ___ your lies, ___ lies, ___ lies. __

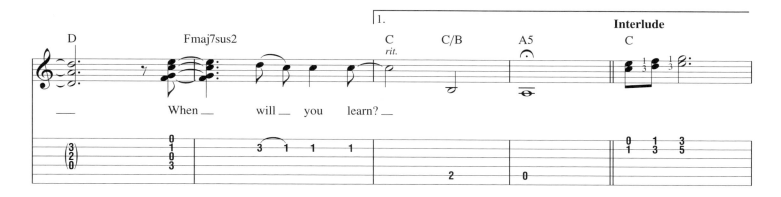

When ___ will ___ you learn? ___

**Interlude**

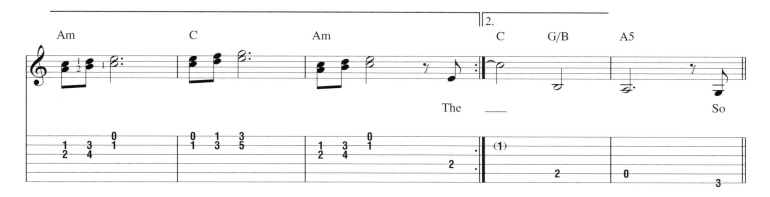

The ___ So

**Outro-Verse**

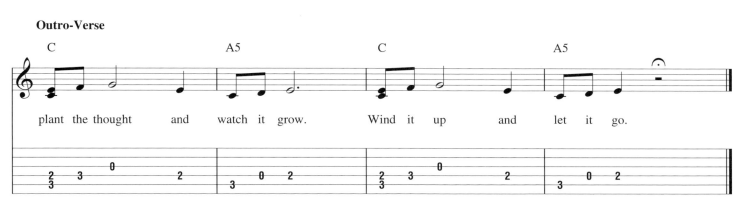

plant the thought and watch it grow. Wind it up and let it go.

# Broken Hearted Hoover
# Fixer Sucker Guy

Words and Music by Glen Hansard

**Chorus**

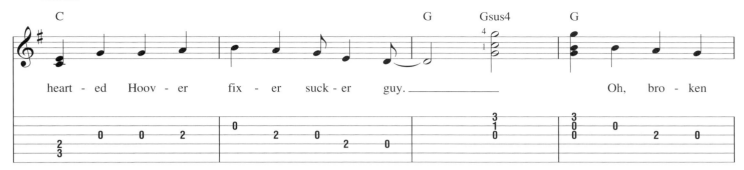

heart - ed Hoov - er fix - er suck - er guy. _____ Oh, bro - ken

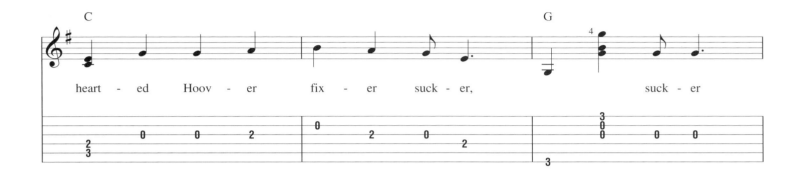

heart - ed Hoov - er fix - er suck - er, suck - er

**Outro-Verse**

guy. One day I'll ___ go there and

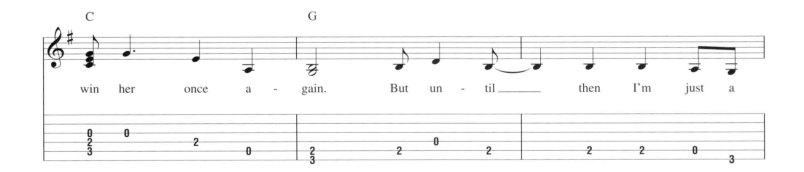

win her once a - gain. But un - til ___ then I'm just a

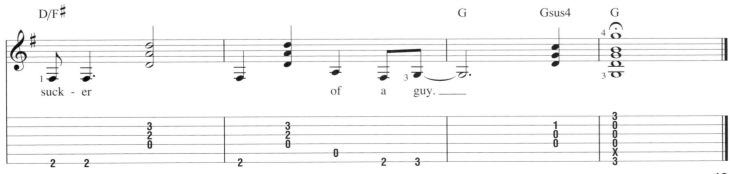

suck - er of a guy. ___

# When Your Mind's Made Up

**Words and Music by Glen Hansard**

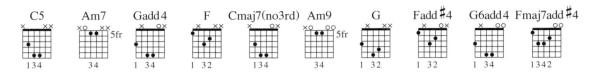

C5    Am7    Gadd4    F    Cmaj7(no3rd)    Am9    G    Fadd#4    G6add4    Fmaj7add#4

**Strum Pattern: 7 & 10**
**Pick Pattern: 7 & 10**

**Intro**
**Fast**

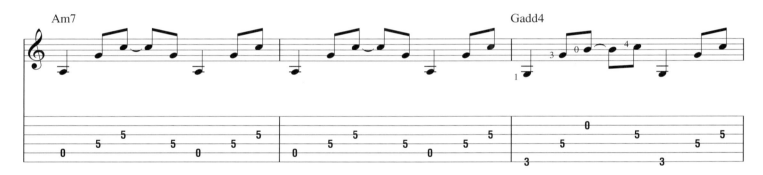

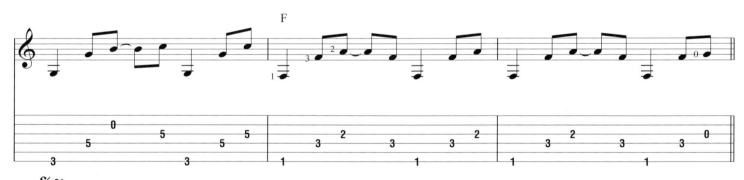

§ **Verse**

*Male:*
1., 3. So
        see,

if  you  ev-er    want some-thin'
you're just  like  ev-'ry - one.

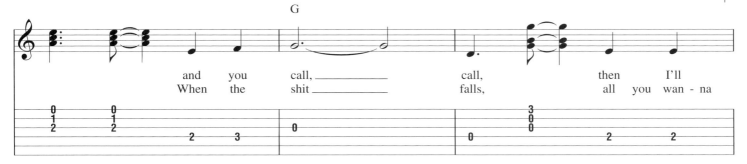

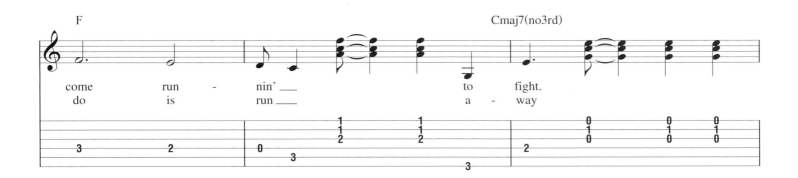

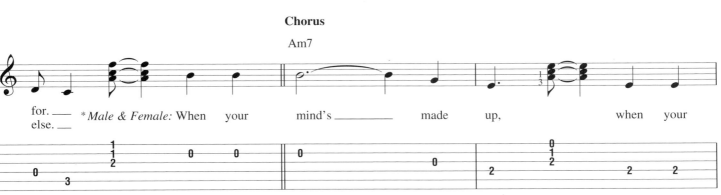

*Hereafter referred to as Both.*

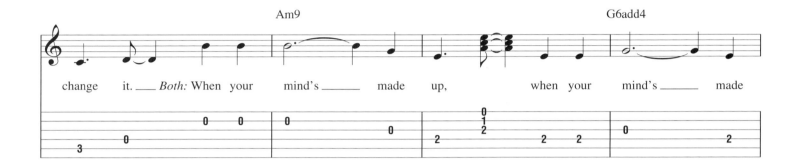

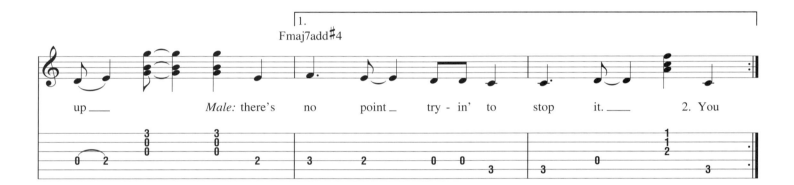

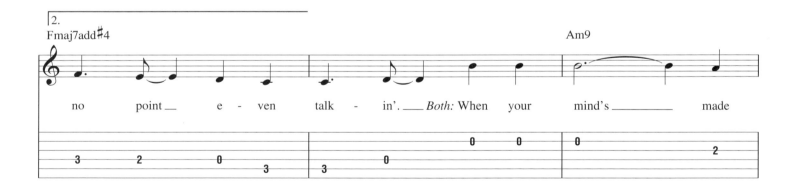

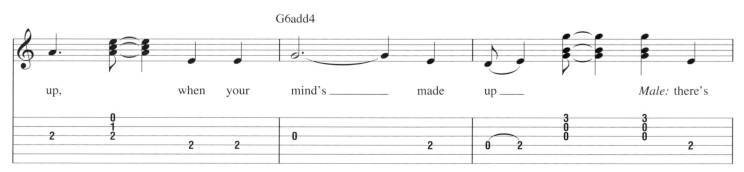

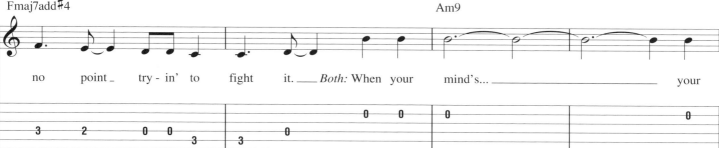

no    point     try - in'  to     fight      it. __ *Both:* When  your     mind's... _____ your

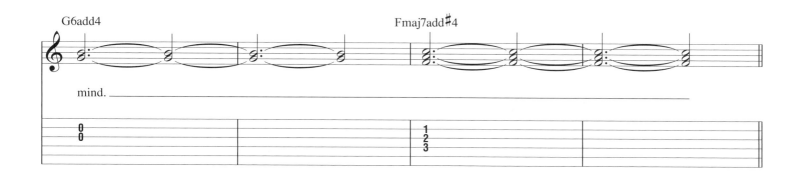

mind. _____

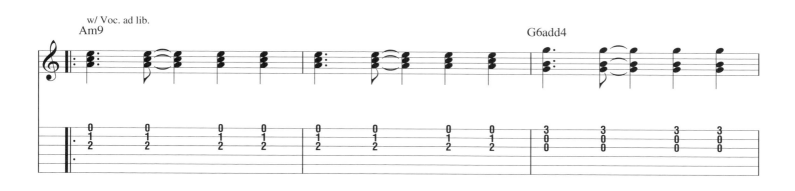

w/ Voc. ad lib.

1. - 4.

5.

***D.S. al Coda***

⊕ **Coda**

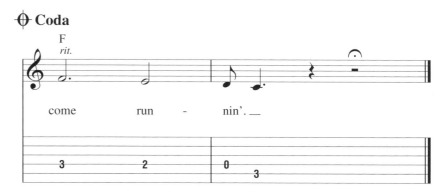

come     run - nin'. __

# Gold

**Words and Music by Fergus O'Farrell**

*Drop D tuning, Capo II
(low to high) D-A-D-G-B-E

**Strum Pattern: 9
**Pick Pattern: 7

Intro
Fast

*Optional: To match recording, place capo at 2nd fret.
**Use Pattern 6 for   meas.

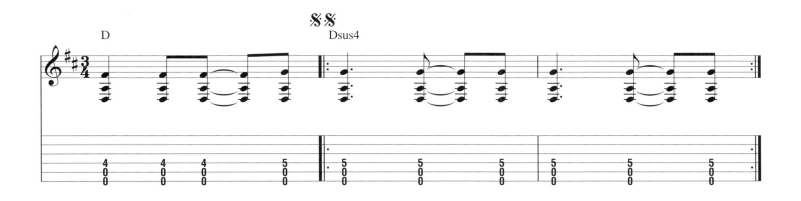

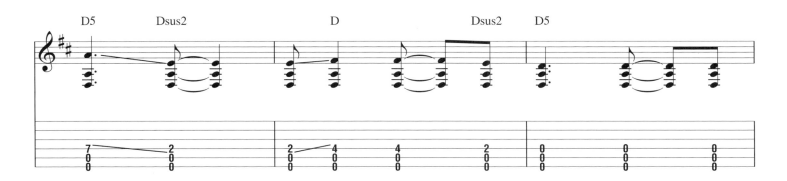

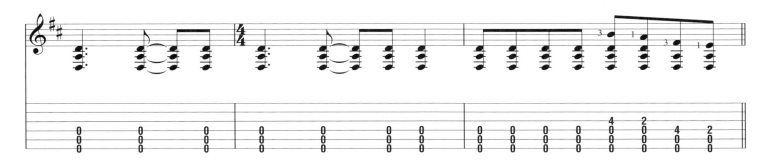

*4th time, To Coda 2* ⊕

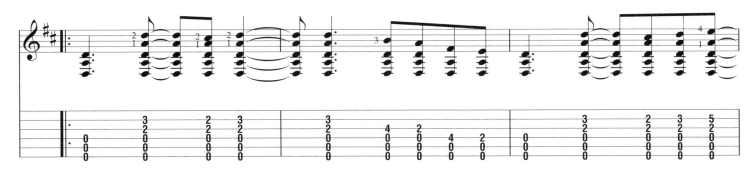

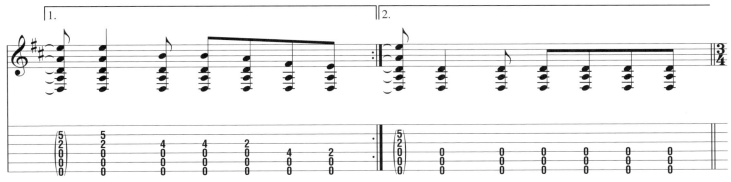

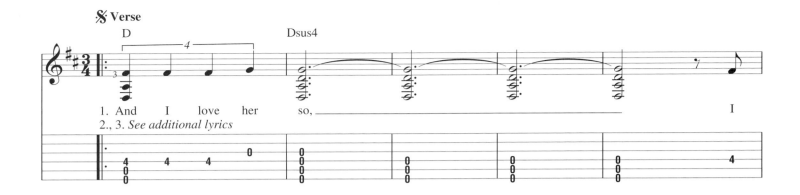

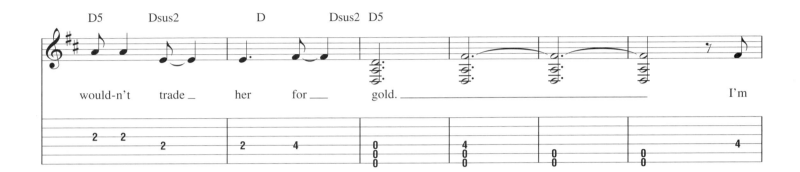

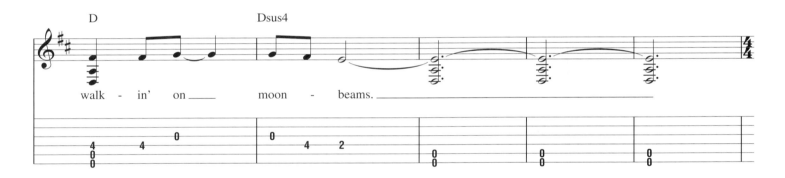

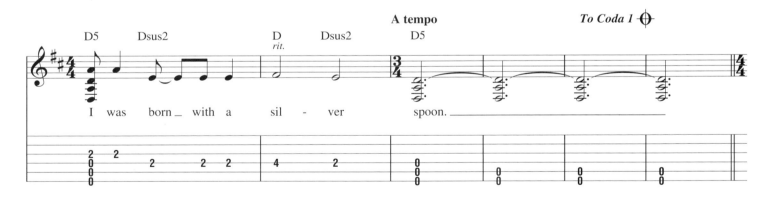

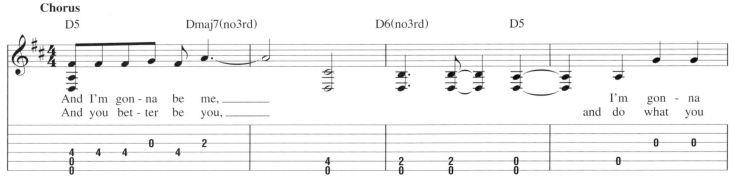

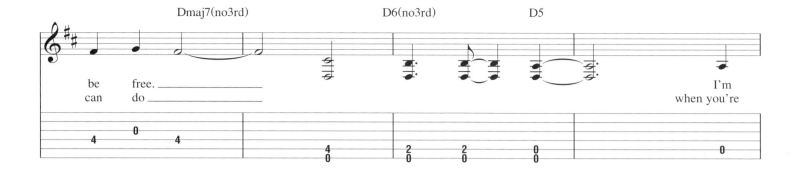

be free. _____

can do _____

I'm

when you're

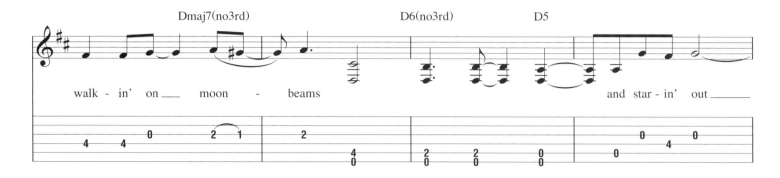

walk - in' on ___ moon - beams

and star - in' out _____

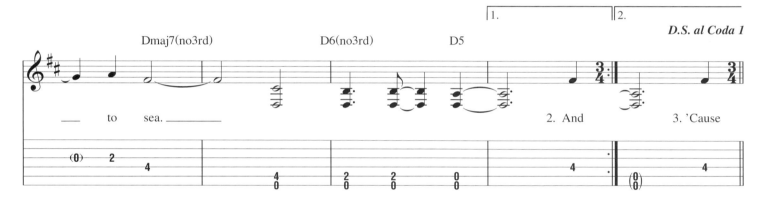

1. | 2.

**D.S. al Coda 1**

___ to sea. _____

2. And

3. 'Cause

⊕ **Coda 1**

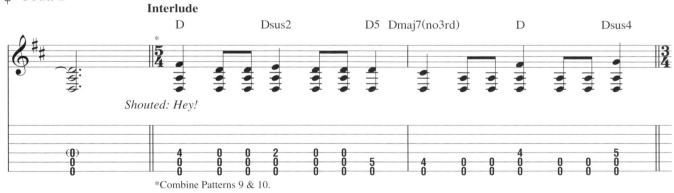

**Interlude**

*Shouted: Hey!*

*Combine Patterns 9 & 10.

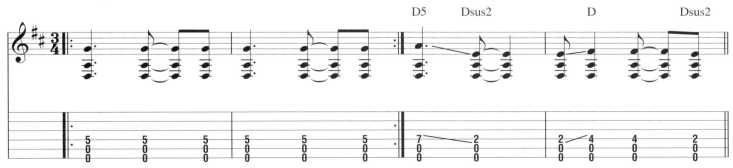

*Shouted: Hey!*

*2nd time.

**D.S.S. al Coda 2**
**(take repeat)**

**⊕ Coda 2**

*Play 3 times*

**Outro-Verse**

And I love her so,_____ I

would-n't trade ___ her _____ for _____ gold._____

*Additional Lyrics*

2. And if a door be closed, then a row of homes start buildin'.
   And tear your curtains down, for sunlight is like gold.

3. 'Cause if your skin was soil, how long do you think before they'd start diggin'?
   And if your life was gold, how long do you think you'd stay livin'?

# All the Way Down

**Words and Music by Glen Hansard**

**Pre-Chorus**

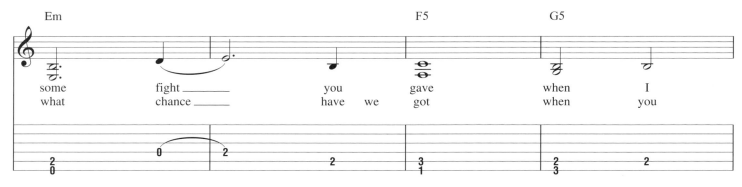

**Chorus**

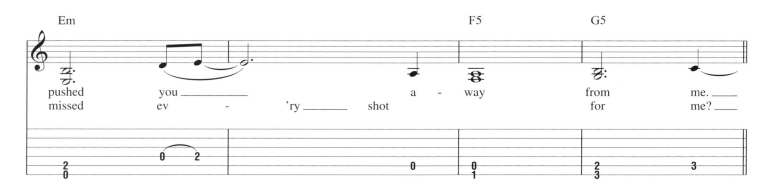

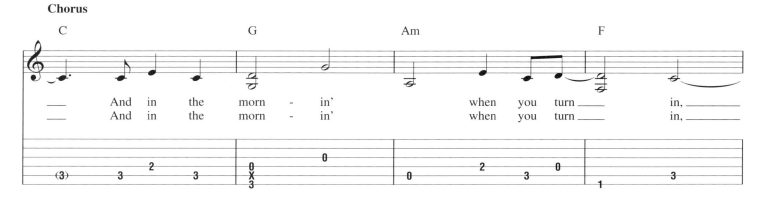

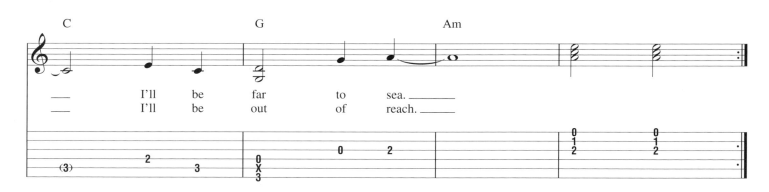

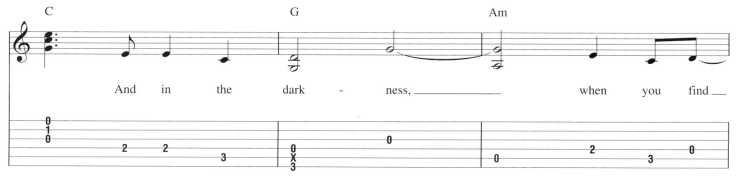

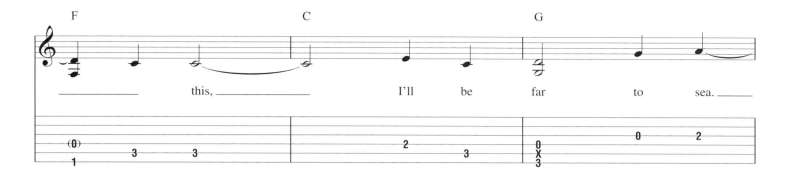

this, _____ _____ I'll be far to sea. _____

**Outro-Verse**

_____ And you have bro - ken me _____ all _____

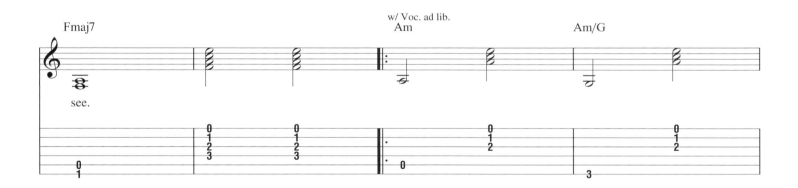

_____ the way _____ down. _____ You'll be the last, you'll

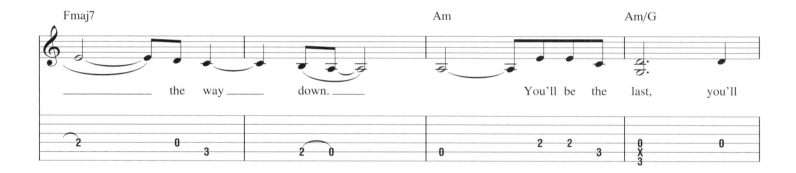

w/ Voc. ad lib.

see.

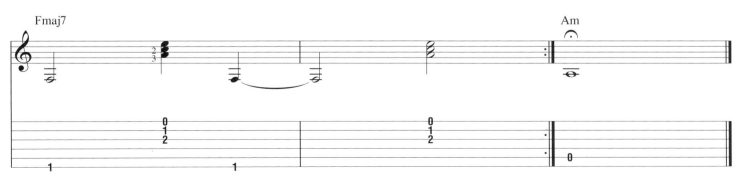

# The Hill

**Words and Music by Marketa Irglova**

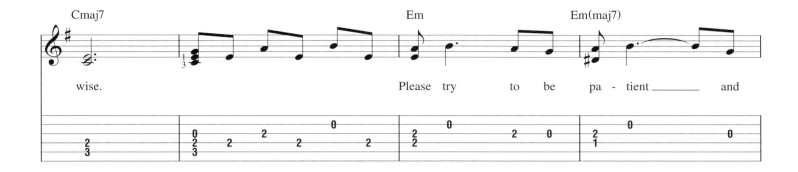

wise.            Please   try   to   be   pa - tient _____ and

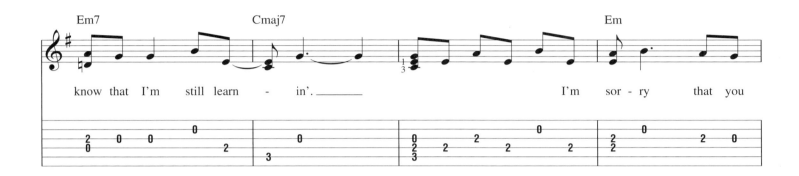

know that I'm still learn - in'. _____          I'm   sor - ry   that you

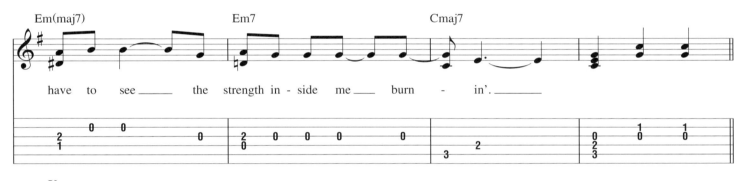

have   to   see _____ the strength in - side me ___ burn - in'. _____

**Verse**

*\*A tempo*

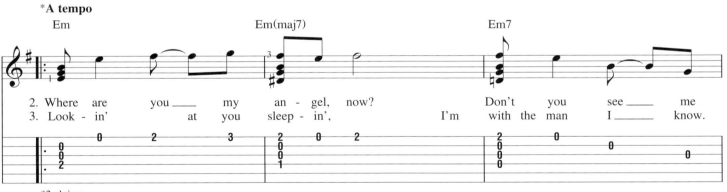

2. Where   are   you ___ my   an - gel,   now?      Don't   you   see ___ me
3. Look - in'     at   you   sleep - in',     I'm   with the man   I _____ know.

*\*2nd time.*

cry - in'? _____                    And   I   know that you ___ can't
                                 I'm   sit - tin' here ___ weep -

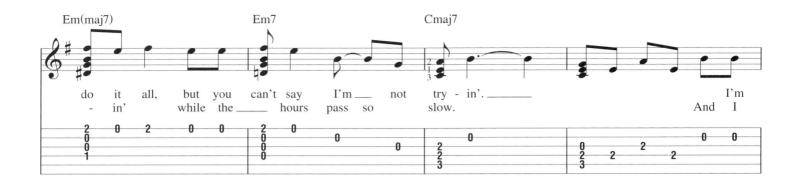

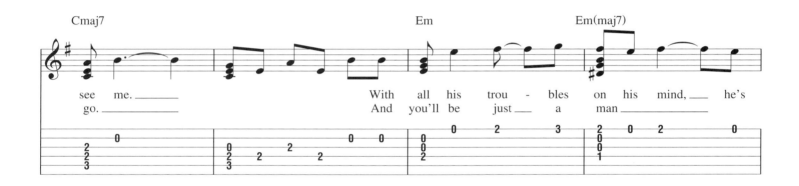

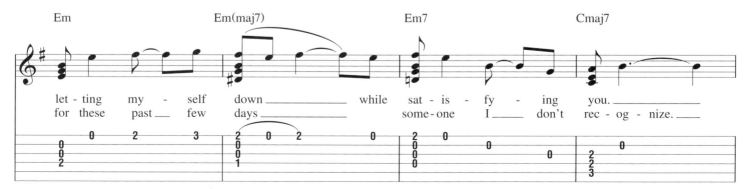

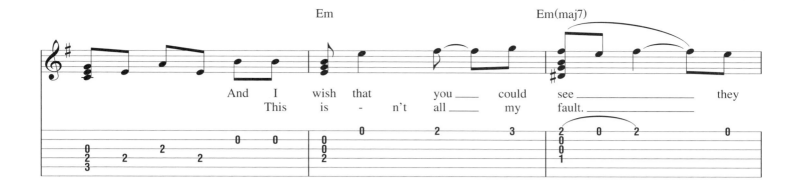

And I wish that you ___ could see _____ they

This is - n't all ___ my fault. _____

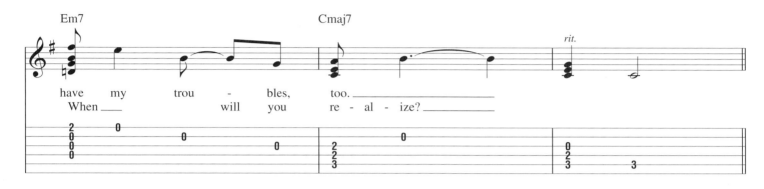

have my trou - bles, too. _____

When ___ will you re - al - ize? _____

**Interlude**

**Faster**

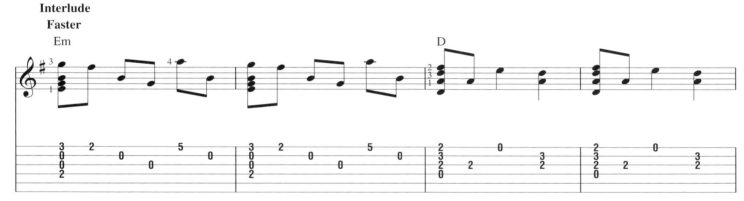

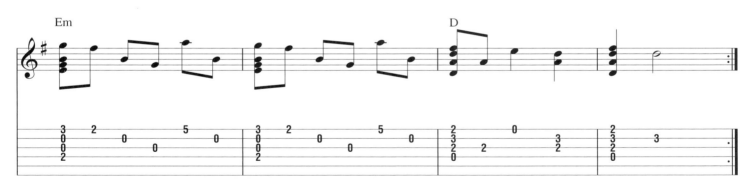

**Outro-Verse**

**A tempo**

Look - in' at you leav - in', _____ I'm look - in' for a sign.

# Fallen from the Sky

**Words and Music by Glen Hansard**

*Capo IV

**Strum Pattern: 5**
**Pick Pattern: 4**

**Intro**
**Moderately**

%. **Chorus**

N.C.
(Drum machine)

*mf* You must have fall-en from the sky.
sky.
sky.

*Optional: To match recording, place capo at 4th fret.

You must have shat-tered on the run - way.
You must have come here in the pour - in' rain.
You must have come here on the wrong ___ way.

You brought so man - y to ___ the light,
You took so man - y through ___ the light,
You came a - mong us ev - 'ry time,

and now you're by your - self. ___
and now you're on your own. ___
but now you're on your own. ___

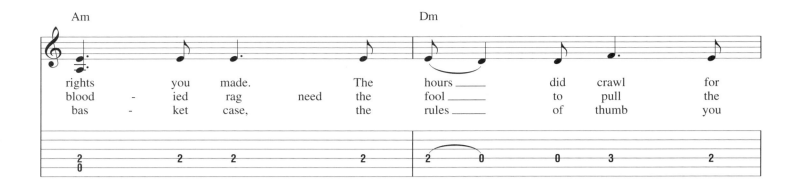

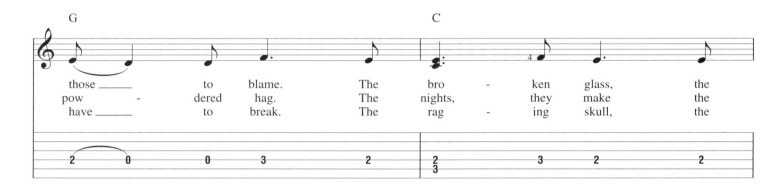

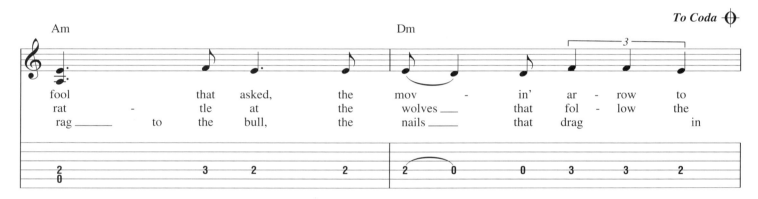

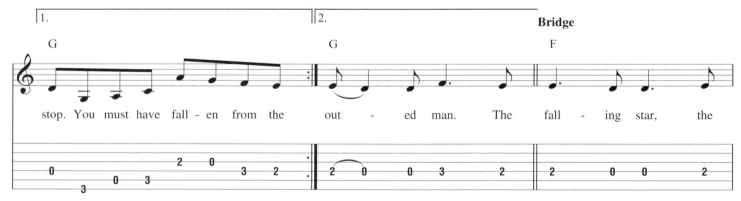

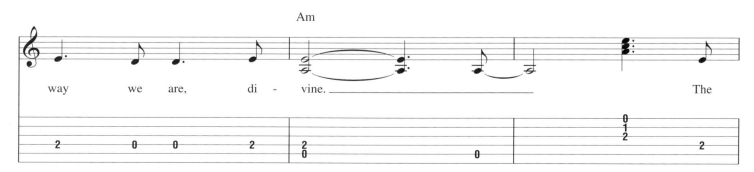

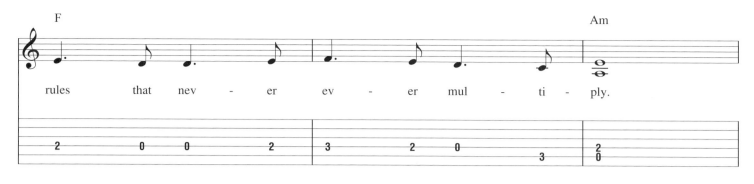

rules that nev - er ev - er mul - ti - ply.

*D.S. al Coda*

**Coda**

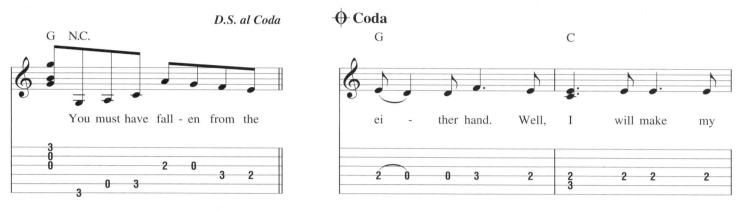

You must have fall - en from the

ei - ther hand. Well, I will make my

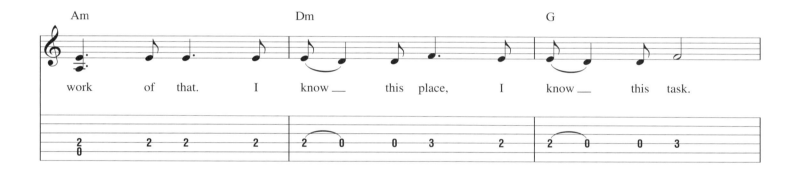

work of that. I know __ this place, I know __ this task.

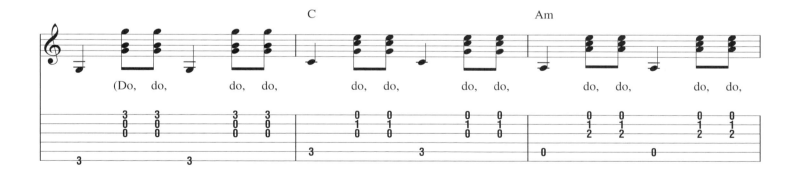

(Do, do, do, do, do, do, do, do, do, do, do, do,

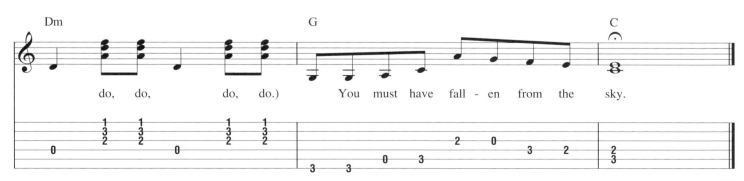

do, do, do, do.) You must have fall - en from the sky.

# Leave

**Words and Music by Glen Hansard**

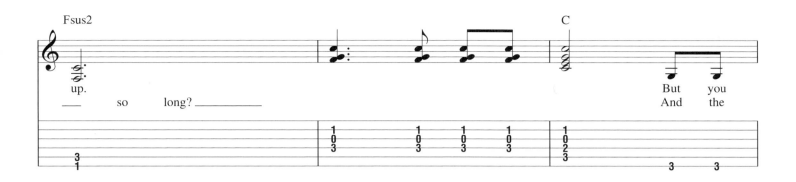

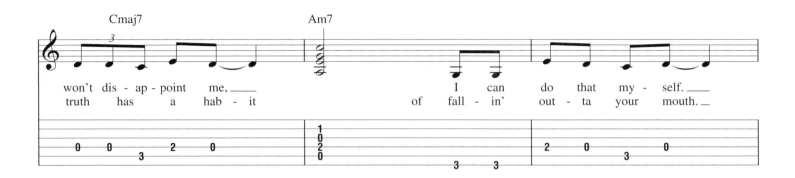

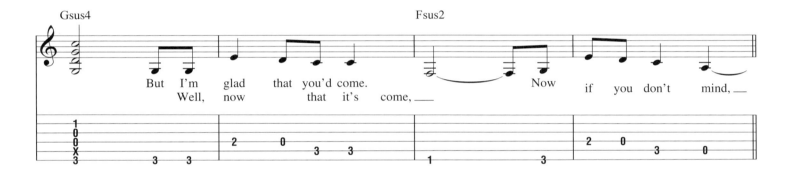

**Chorus**

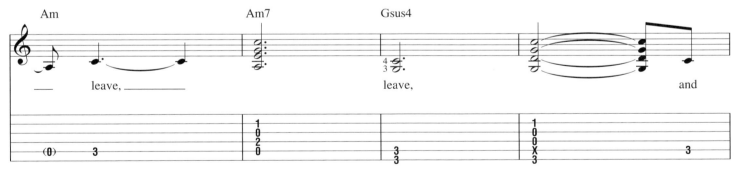

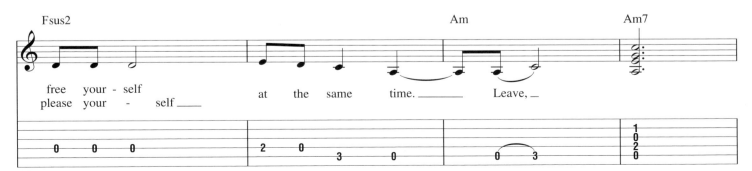

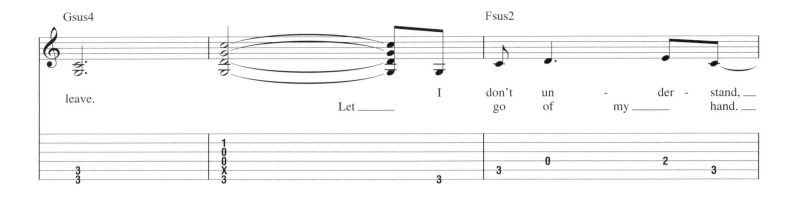

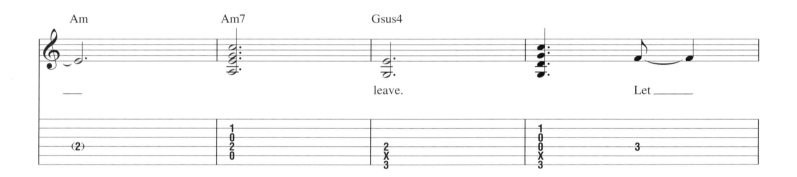

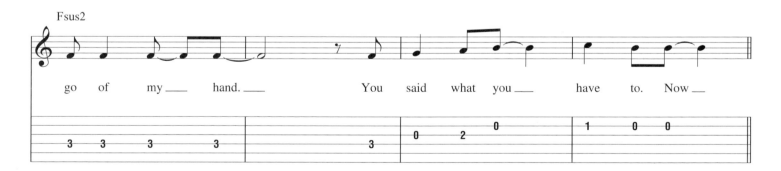

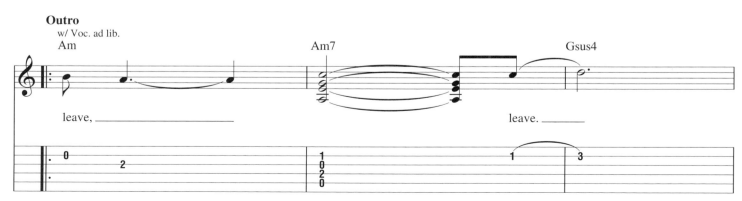

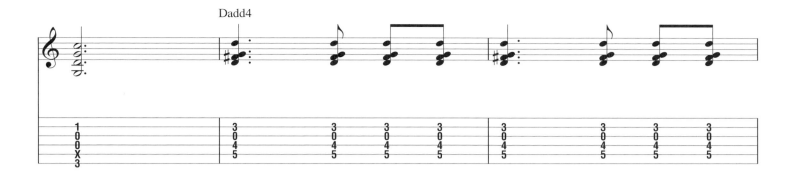

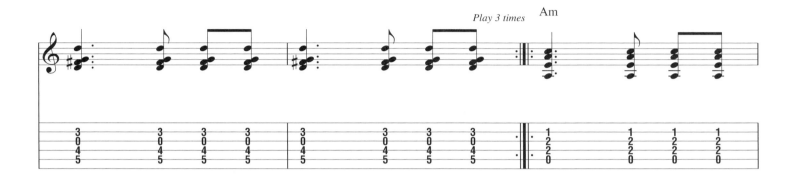

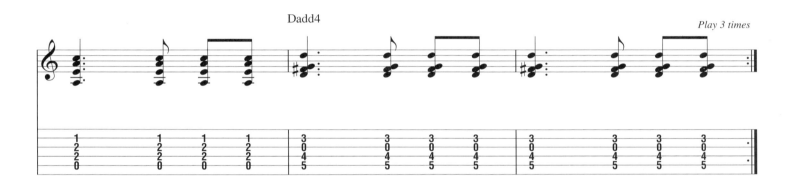

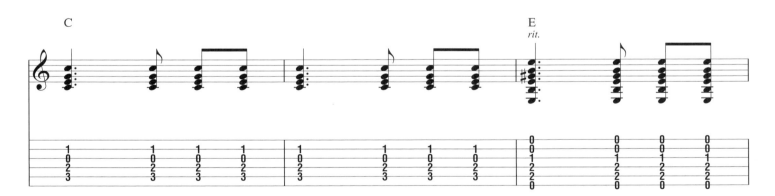

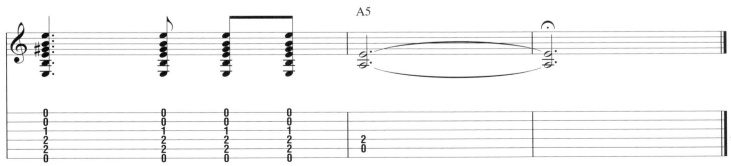

# Trying to Pull Myself Away

**Words and Music by Glen Hansard**

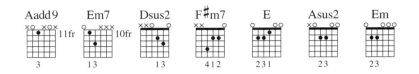

**Strum Pattern: 5**
**Pick Pattern: 1**

**Verse**
**Moderately**

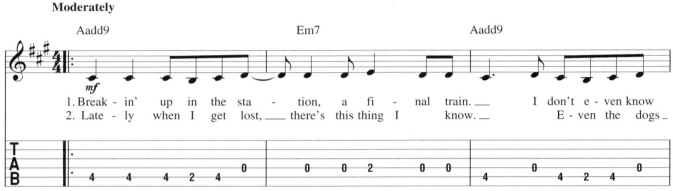

1. Break - in' up in the sta - tion, a fi - nal train.___ I don't e - ven know
2. Late - ly when I get lost,___ there's this thing I know.___ E - ven the dogs___

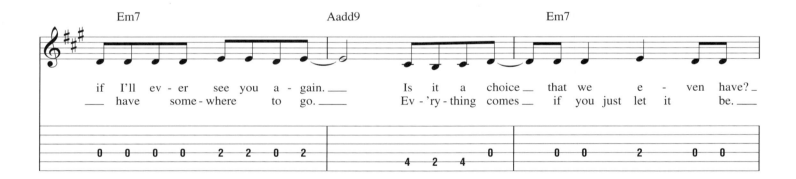

if I'll ev - er see you a - gain.___ Is it a choice___ that we e - ven have?___
___ have some - where to go.___ Ev - 'ry - thing comes___ if you just let it be.___

Bang, bang down on pi - a -
Work, work, bright - en the corn -

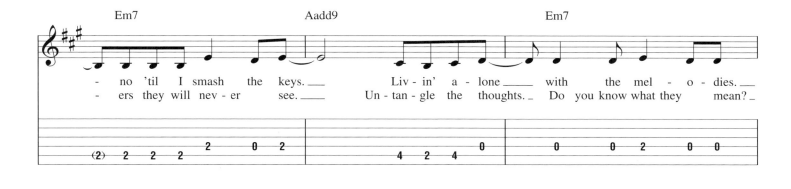

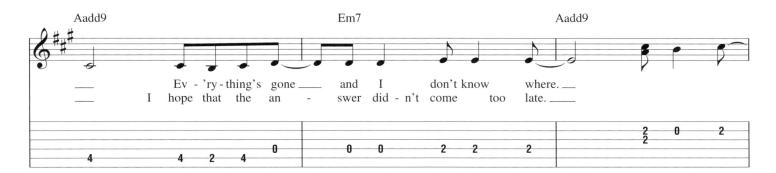

**Pre-Chorus**

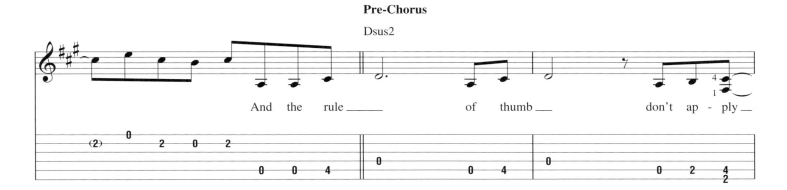

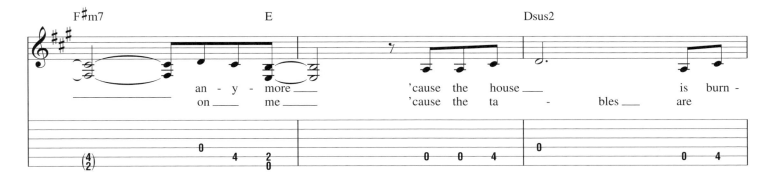

**Chorus**

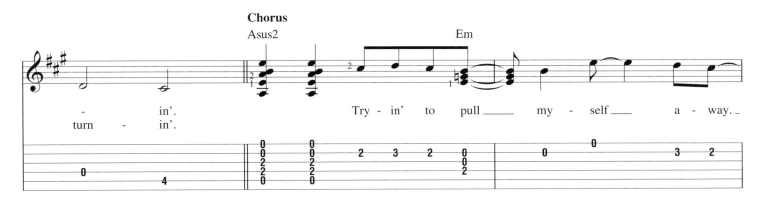

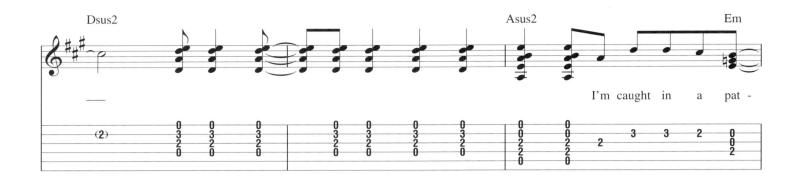

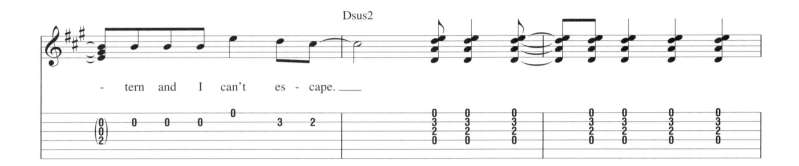

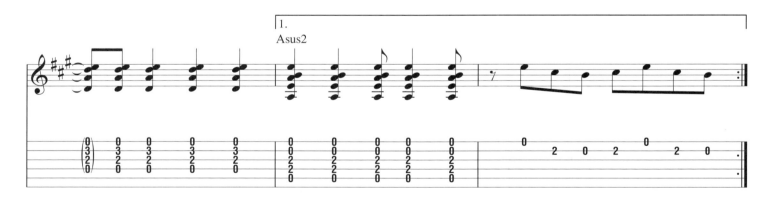

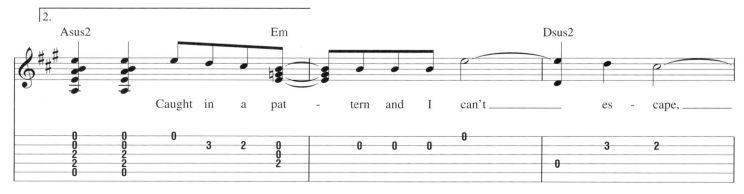

# Once

**Words and Music by Glen Hansard**

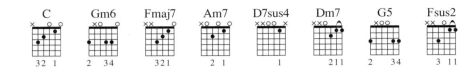

**Strum Pattern: 7**
**Pick Pattern: 7**

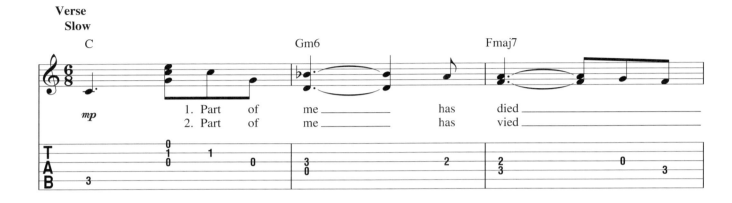

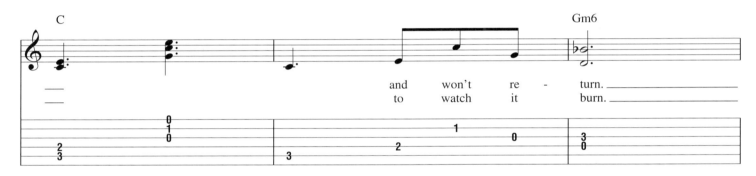

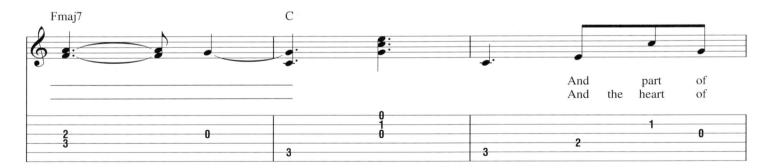

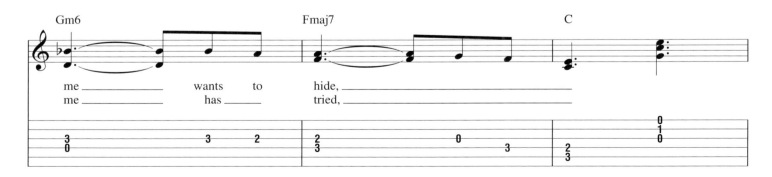

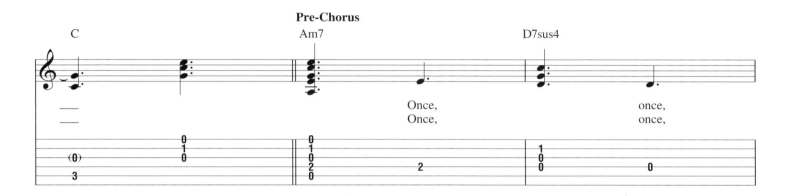

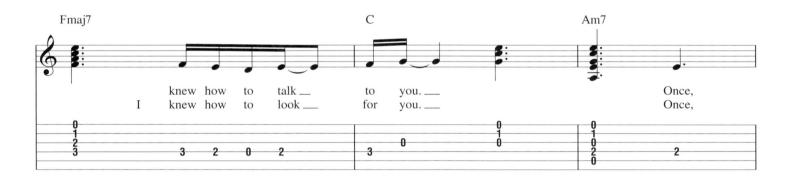

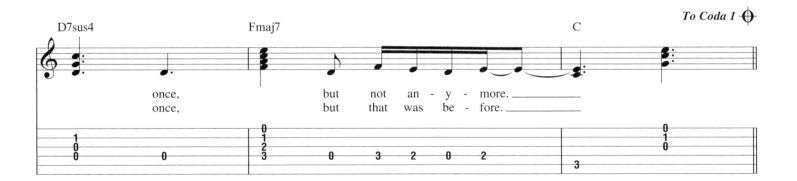

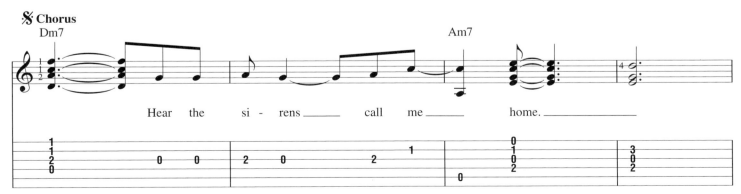

Dm7                                     Am7

Hear the si - rens _____ call me _____ home. _____

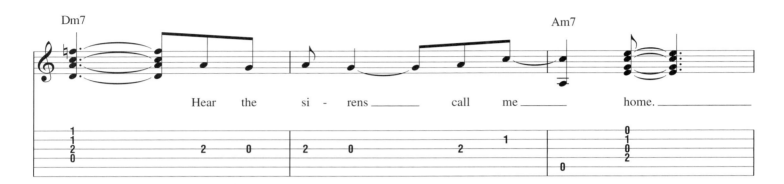

Dm7                                     Am7

Hear the si - rens _____ call me _____ home. _____

*To Coda 2*

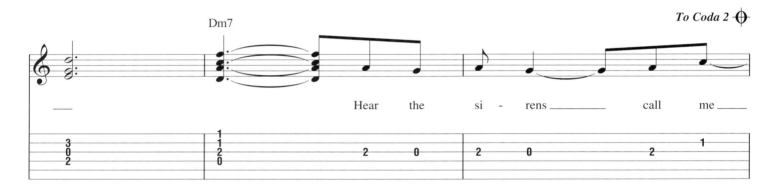

Dm7

_____ Hear the si - rens _____ call me _____

*D.C. al Coda 1*           **Coda 1**

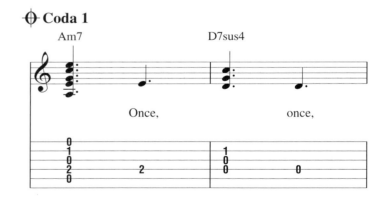

Am7                            Am7                D7sus4

_____ home. _____                          Once,        once,

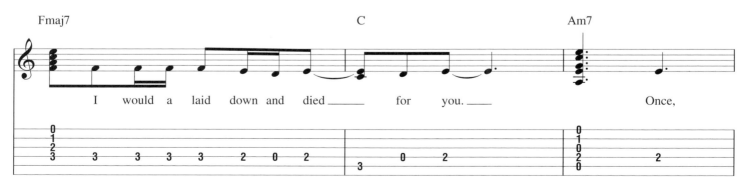

Fmaj7                                    C                        Am7

I would a laid down and died _____ for you. _____           Once,

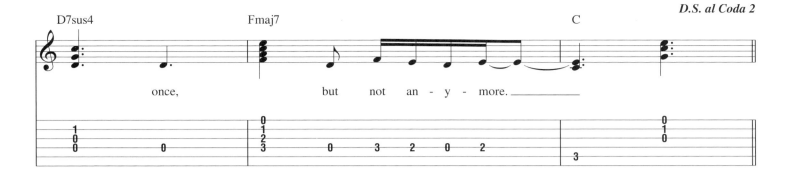

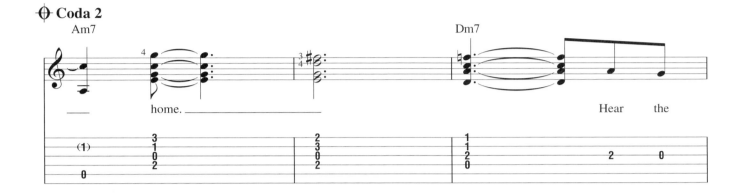

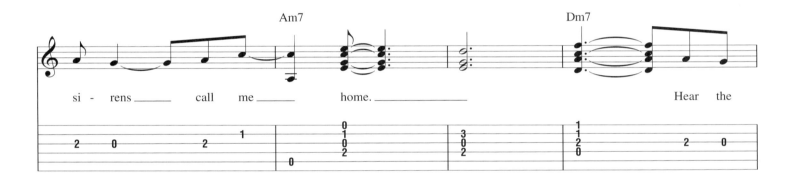

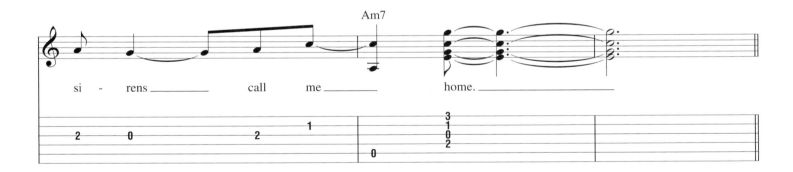

**Outro**

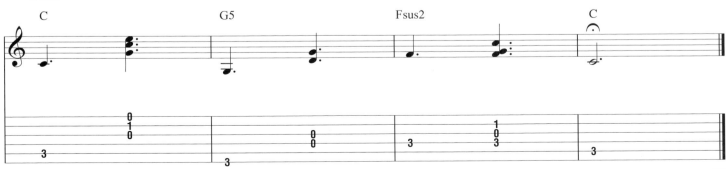

# Say It to Me Now

**Words and Music by Glen Hansard, Graham Downey, Paul Brennan,
Noreen O'Donnell, Colm Macconiomaire and David Odlum**

**Strum Pattern: 2**
**Pick Pattern: 2**

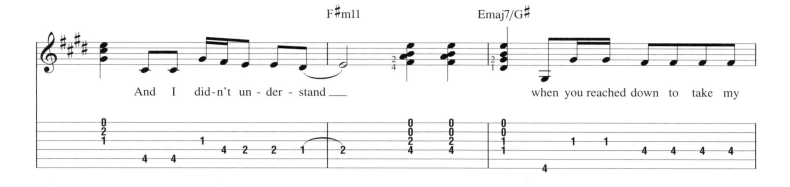

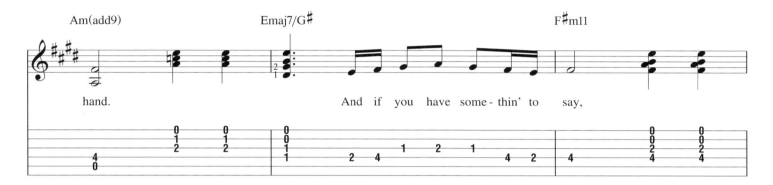

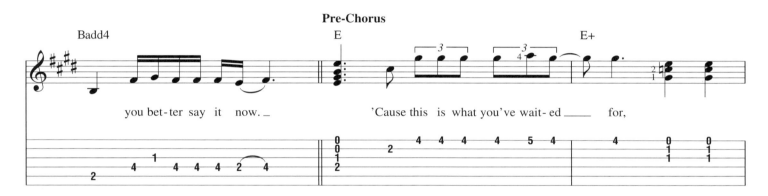

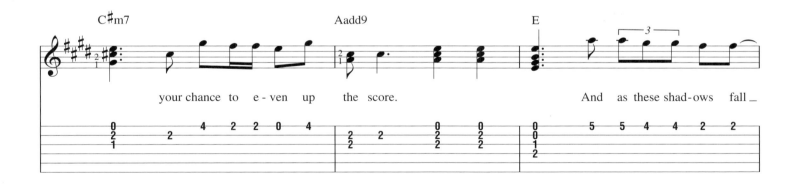

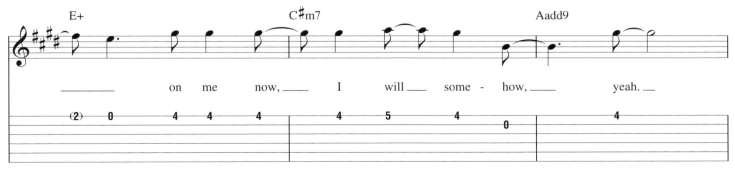

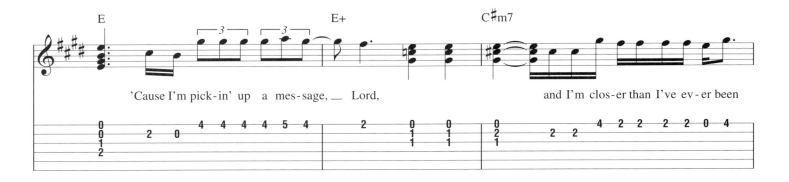

'Cause I'm pick-in' up a mes-sage, __ Lord, and I'm clos-er than I've ev-er been

**Chorus**

be - fore. So if you have some-thin' to ____ say, say it to me now. __

Just say it to me now, _____ now. __

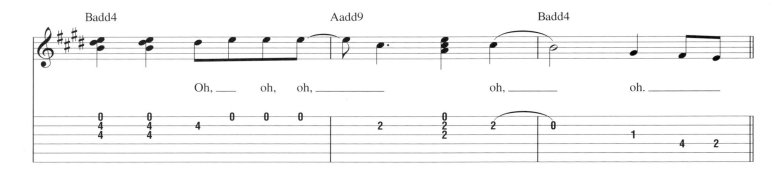

Oh, __ oh, oh, _____ oh, _____ oh. _____

**Outro**